This Book Belongs to:

· · · · · · · · · · · · · · · · · · · ·

· · · · · · · · · · · · · · · · · · · ·

Week

This Week I'm looking forward to:

Monday

Today I'm thankful for:

Tuesday

Today I'm thankful for:

Wednesday

Today I'm thankful for:

1

Today I'm thankful for:

Thursday

Today I'm thankful for:

Friday

Today I'm thankful for:

Sunday

Today I'm thankful for:

Saturday

Small Acts of Kindness I can do this week:

Weekly Assignment:
What is the best gift I've ever been given and why did it mean so much?

Week

"He Is My strength, my shield from every danger. I trusted in Him, and He helped me. Joy rises in my heart until I burst out into songs of praise to Him."

- Psalm 28:7 (TLB)

This Week I'm looking forward to:

Monday
Today I'm thankful for:

Tuesday
Today I'm thankful for:

Wednesday
Today I'm thankful for:

2

Today I'm thankful for:

Thursday

Today I'm thankful for:

Friday

Today I'm thankful for:

Sunday

Today I'm thankful for:

Saturday

Small Acts of Kindness I can do this week:

Weekly Assignment:

Write about a person who has really helped me and what they did:

Week

Weekly Inspiration:

"Gratitude helps me focus on what I have instead of what I don't have, allowing me to stay focused on my blessings instead of worrying."

— Joyce Meyer, The Power of being Thankful

This Week I'm looking forward to:

Monday
Today I'm thankful for:

Tuesday
Today I'm thankful for:

Wednesday
Today I'm thankful for:

3

Today I'm thankful for:

Thursday

Today I'm thankful for:

Friday

Today I'm thankful for:

Sunday

Today I'm thankful for:

Saturday

Small Acts of Kindness I can do this week:

Weekly Assignment:

What is something positive I'm learning through a rough situation:

Week

Weekly Inspiration:

"All This is for your benefit, so that the grace that is reaching more and more people may cause thanksgiving to overflow to the glory of God... And as God's grace reaches more and more people there will be great thanksgiving, and God will receive more and more glory."
-2 Cor. 4:15 (NIV)

This Week I'm looking forward to:

Monday

Today I'm thankful for:

Tuesday

Today I'm thankful for:

Wednesday

Today I'm thankful for:

4

Today I'm thankful for:

Thursday

Today I'm thankful for:

Friday

Today I'm thankful for:

Sunday

Today I'm thankful for:

Saturday

Small Acts of Kindness I can do this week:

Weekly Assignment:
Who are the people I can't imagine doing life without, and why?

Week

This Week I'm looking forward to:

Monday

Today I'm thankful for:

Tuesday

Today I'm thankful for:

Wednesday

Today I'm thankful for:

5

Today I'm thankful for:

Thursday

Today I'm thankful for:

Friday

Today I'm thankful for:

Sunday

Today I'm thankful for:

Saturday

Small Acts of Kindness I can do this week:

Weekly Assignment:

What are 3 qualities I admire about a person that sometimes annoys me:

Week

"[we pray that you may be] strengthened and invigorated with all the power, according to His glorious might, to attain every kind of endurance and patience with joy; giving thanks to the Father, who has qualified us to share in the inheritance of the saints (God's people) in the Light."
-Col. 1:11-12 (AMP)

This Week I'm looking forward to:

Monday
Today I'm thankful for:

Tuesday
Today I'm thankful for:

Wednesday
Today I'm thankful for:

6

Today I'm thankful for:

Thursday

Today I'm thankful for:

Friday

Today I'm thankful for:

Sunday

Today I'm thankful for:

Saturday

Small Acts of Kindness I can do this week:

Weekly Assignment:

What matters most to me in this life?

Weekly Inspiration:

"Great is Thy faithfulness!
Great is Thy faithfulness!
Morning by morning new
mercies I see;
All I have needed Thy hand
hath provided-
Great is Thy faithfulness, Lord
unto me!"

-Thomas Chisholm (hymn
"Great is Thy Faithfulness")

Week

This Week I'm looking
forward to:

Today I'm thankful for:

Monday

Today I'm thankful for:

Tuesday

Today I'm thankful for:

Wednesday

7

Today I'm thankful for:

Thursday

Today I'm thankful for:

Friday

Today I'm thankful for:

Sunday

Today I'm thankful for:

Saturday

Small Acts of Kindness I can do this week:

Weekly Assignment:

Remember a situation where God made a way when it seemed hopeless.

Week

Weekly Inspiration:

"When I started counting my blessings, my whole life turned around."

- Willie Nelson

This Week I'm looking forward to:

Monday

Today I'm thankful for:

Tuesday

Today I'm thankful for:

Wednesday

Today I'm thankful for:

8

Today I'm thankful for:

Thursday

Today I'm thankful for:

Friday

Today I'm thankful for:

Sunday

Today I'm thankful for:

Saturday

Small Acts of Kindness I can do this week:

Weekly Assignment:

Write a list of characteristics I like about myself:

Weekly Inspiration:

"The LORD is my strength and my shield; my heart trusts in Him, and He helps me. My heart leaps for joy, and with my song I praise Him."

-Psalm 28;7 (NIV)

This Week I'm looking forward to:

Monday

Today I'm thankful for:

Tuesday

Today I'm thankful for:

Wednesday

Today I'm thankful for:

9

Today I'm thankful for:

Thursday

Today I'm thankful for:

Friday

Today I'm thankful for:

Sunday

Today I'm thankful for:

Saturday

Small Acts of Kindness I can do this week:

Weekly Assignment:

Forgive myself and let go.

Weekly Inspiration:

"Let gratitude be the pillow upon which you kneel to say your nightly prayer. And let faith be the bridge you build to overcome evil and welcome good.

— Maya Angelou, Celebrations: Rituals of Peace and Prayer

This Week I'm looking forward to:

Monday

Today I'm thankful for:

Tuesday

Today I'm thankful for:

Wednesday

Today I'm thankful for:

10

Today I'm thankful for:

Thursday

Today I'm thankful for:

Friday

Today I'm thankful for:

Sunday

Today I'm thankful for:

Saturday

Small Acts of Kindness I can do this week:

Weekly Assignment:

Who is the person I feel the most loved by and why?

Weekly Inspiration:

"As we express our gratitude, we must never forget that the highest appreciation is not to utter words, but to live by them."

-John F. Kennedy

This Week I'm looking forward to:

Monday

Today I'm thankful for:

Tuesday

Today I'm thankful for:

Wednesday

Today I'm thankful for:

11

Today I'm thankful for:

Thursday

Today I'm thankful for:

Friday

Today I'm thankful for:

Sunday

Today I'm thankful for:

Saturday

Small Acts of Kindness I can do this week:

Weekly Assignment:

What is the best thing that's ever happened to me?

Week

Weekly Inspiration:

"The steadfast love of the Lord never ceases, His mercies never come to an end, they are new every morning; great is your faithfulness."

-Lamentations 3;22-23

This Week I'm looking forward to:

Monday

Today I'm thankful for:

Tuesday

Today I'm thankful for:

Wednesday

Today I'm thankful for:

12

Today I'm thankful for:

Thursday

Today I'm thankful for:

Friday

Today I'm thankful for:

Sunday

Today I'm thankful for:

Saturday

Small Acts of Kindness I can do this week:

Weekly Assignment:

Write a list of things that make me smile:

Weekly Inspiration:

"Enjoy the little things, for one day you may look back and realize they were the big things."

–Robert Brault

This Week I'm looking forward to:

Monday

Today I'm thankful for:

Tuesday

Today I'm thankful for:

Wednesday

Today I'm thankful for:

13

Today I'm thankful for:

Thursday

Today I'm thankful for:

Friday

Today I'm thankful for:

Sunday

Today I'm thankful for:

Saturday

Small Acts of Kindness I can do this week:

Weekly Assignment:

What is an accomplishment I'm proud of?

Week

"Sometimes,' said Pooh, 'the smallest things take up the most room in your heart."

-A.A. Milne

This Week I'm looking forward to:

Monday

Today I'm thankful for:

Tuesday

Today I'm thankful for:

Wednesday

Today I'm thankful for:

14

Today I'm thankful for:

Thursday

Today I'm thankful for:

Friday

Today I'm thankful for:

Sunday

Today I'm thankful for:

Saturday

Small Acts of Kindness I can do this week:

Weekly Assignment:

Write about a memory that

makes me feel happy.:

Week

"The best and most beautiful things in the world cannot be seen or even touched – they must be felt with the heart."

-Helen Keller

This Week I'm looking forward to:

Monday
Today I'm thankful for:

Tuesday
Today I'm thankful for:

Wednesday
Today I'm thankful for:

15

Today I'm thankful for:

Thursday

Today I'm thankful for:

Friday

Today I'm thankful for:

Sunday

Today I'm thankful for:

Saturday

Small Acts of Kindness I can do this week:

Weekly Assignment:

Send a note or message to someone I'm thankful for.

Week

"I am not afraid of storms, for I am learning how to sail my ship."

-Louisa May Alcott, Little Women

This Week I'm looking forward to:

Monday

Today I'm thankful for:

Tuesday

Today I'm thankful for:

Wednesday

Today I'm thankful for:

16

Today I'm thankful for:

Thursday

Today I'm thankful for:

Friday

Today I'm thankful for:

Sunday

Today I'm thankful for:

Saturday

Small Acts of Kindness I can do this week:

Weekly Assignment:

What's a difficult hurdle in my life

that I've overcome:

Week

"The thankful receiver bears a plentiful harvest."

-William Blake

This Week I'm looking forward to:

Monday

Today I'm thankful for:

Tuesday

Today I'm thankful for:

Wednesday

Today I'm thankful for:

17

Today I'm thankful for:

Thursday

Today I'm thankful for:

Friday

Today I'm thankful for:

Sunday

Today I'm thankful for:

Saturday

Small Acts of Kindness I can do this week:

Weekly Assignment:

What's something I have now that used to be something I only dreamed of?

Week

"Finally, brothers and sisters, whatever is true, whatever is noble, whatever is right, whatever is pure, whatever is lovely, whatever is admirable - if anything is excellent or praiseworthy - think about such things."

-Philippians 4:8 (NIV)

This Week I'm looking forward to:

Monday
Today I'm thankful for:

Tuesday
Today I'm thankful for:

Wednesday
Today I'm thankful for:

18

Today I'm thankful for:

Thursday

Today I'm thankful for:

Friday

Today I'm thankful for:

Sunday

Today I'm thankful for:

Saturday

Small Acts of Kindness I can do this week:

Weekly Assignment:

What are some things that help me feel relaxed and calm?

How can I incorporate some of these things into my week?

Week

Weekly Inspiration:

"If more of us valued food and cheer and song above hoarded gold, it would be a merrier world."

— J.R.R. Tolkien, The Hobbit, or There and Back Again

This Week I'm looking forward to:

Monday

Today I'm thankful for:

Tuesday

Today I'm thankful for:

Wednesday

Today I'm thankful for:

19

Today I'm thankful for:

Thursday

Today I'm thankful for:

Friday

Today I'm thankful for:

Today I'm thankful for:

Sunday

Saturday

Small Acts of Kindness I can do this week:

Weekly Assignment:

Write about my favorite thing to see in nature (Sky, mountain, trees, etc.) and how it makes me feel:

Week

Weekly Inspiration:

"Let the peace of Christ [the inner calm of one who walks daily with Him] be the controlling factor in your hearts [deciding and settling questions that arise]. To this peace indeed you were called as members in one body [of believers]. And be thankful [to God always]."

-Colossians 3:15 (AMP)

This Week I'm looking forward to:

Monday
Today I'm thankful for:

Tuesday
Today I'm thankful for:

Wednesday
Today I'm thankful for:

20

Today I'm thankful for:

Thursday

Today I'm thankful for:

Friday

Today I'm thankful for:

Sunday

Today I'm thankful for:

Saturday

Small Acts of Kindness I can do this week:

Weekly Assignment:

What's the best advice I've ever received and who gave it?

Week

This Week I'm looking forward to:

Monday

Today I'm thankful for:

Tuesday

Today I'm thankful for:

Wednesday

Today I'm thankful for:

21

Today I'm thankful for:

Thursday

Today I'm thankful for:

Friday

Today I'm thankful for:

Sunday

Today I'm thankful for:

Saturday

Small Acts of Kindness I can do this week:

Weekly Assignment:

What 3 things do I like most about my family?

Weekly Inspiration:

"God never made a promise that was too good to be true."

-Dwight L. Moody

This Week I'm looking forward to:

Monday

Today I'm thankful for:

Tuesday

Today I'm thankful for:

Wednesday

Today I'm thankful for:

22

Thursday

Today I'm thankful for:

Friday

Today I'm thankful for:

Sunday

Today I'm thankful for:

Saturday

Today I'm thankful for:

Small Acts of Kindness I can do this week:

Weekly Assignment:

What's a hope or dream I have for this next year:

Week

"Keep your eyes open to your mercies. The man who forgets to be thankful has fallen asleep in life."

-Robert Louis Stevenson

This Week I'm looking forward to:

Monday
Today I'm thankful for:

Tuesday
Today I'm thankful for:

Wednesday
Today I'm thankful for:

23

Today I'm thankful for:

Thursday

Today I'm thankful for:

Friday

Today I'm thankful for:

Sunday

Today I'm thankful for:

Saturday

Small Acts of Kindness I can do this week:

Weekly Assignment:

Looking around me now, what are 3 tangible things that help me or improve my life in some way?

Weekly Inspiration:

"Let us always meet each other with smile, for the smile is the beginning of love."

- Mother Teresa

This Week I'm looking forward to:

Monday

Today I'm thankful for:

Tuesday

Today I'm thankful for:

Wednesday

Today I'm thankful for:

24

Today I'm thankful for:

Thursday

Today I'm thankful for:

Friday

Today I'm thankful for:

Sunday

Today I'm thankful for:

Saturday

Small Acts of Kindness I can do this week:

Weekly Assignment:

Something that always makes me laugh:

Weekly Inspiration:

"Some people are always grumbling because roses have thorns, I am thankful that thorns have roses."

-Alphonse Karr

Week

This Week I'm looking forward to:

Monday

Today I'm thankful for:

Tuesday

Today I'm thankful for:

Wednesday

Today I'm thankful for:

25

Today I'm thankful for:

Thursday

Today I'm thankful for:

Friday

Today I'm thankful for:

Sunday

Today I'm thankful for:

Saturday

Small Acts of Kindness I can do this week:

Weekly Assignment:

Write about a mentor I'm thankful for and how he/she has impacted me:

Weekly Inspiration:

"You will be enriched in every way so that you can be generous on every occasion, and through us your generosity will result in thanksgiving to God."

-2Corinthians 9:11 (NIV)

This Week I'm looking forward to:

Monday
Today I'm thankful for:

Tuesday
Today I'm thankful for:

Wednesday
Today I'm thankful for:

26

Thursday

Today I'm thankful for:

Friday

Today I'm thankful for:

Sunday

Today I'm thankful for:

Saturday

Today I'm thankful for:

Small Acts of Kindness I can do this week:

Weekly Assignment:

3 things I most appreciate about my significant other or my best friend:

Week

Weekly Inspiration:

"Gratitude is the fairest blossom which springs from the soul."

-Henry Ward Beecher

This Week I'm looking forward to:

Monday
Today I'm thankful for:

Tuesday
Today I'm thankful for:

Wednesday
Today I'm thankful for:

27

Today I'm thankful for:

Thursday

Today I'm thankful for:

Friday

Today I'm thankful for:

Sunday

Today I'm thankful for:

Saturday

Small Acts of Kindness I can do this week:

Weekly Assignment:

Take a moment to reflect God's presence and goodness in my life.

Weekly Inspiration:

"You are never too old to set another goal or to dream a new dream."

-C.S. Lewis

This Week I'm looking forward to:

Today I'm thankful for:

Monday

Today I'm thankful for:

Tuesday

Today I'm thankful for:

Wednesday

28

Today I'm thankful for:

Thursday

Today I'm thankful for:

Friday

Today I'm thankful for:

Sunday

Today I'm thankful for:

Saturday

Small Acts of Kindness I can do this week:

Weekly Assignment:

What brings me peace? How can I carry that with me through my day?

Weekly Inspiration:

"Gratitude makes sense of our past, brings peace for today, and creates vision for tomorrow."

-Melody Beattie

This Week I'm looking forward to:

Monday

Today I'm thankful for:

Tuesday

Today I'm thankful for:

Wednesday

Today I'm thankful for:

29

Today I'm thankful for:

Thursday

Today I'm thankful for:

Friday

Today I'm thankful for:

Sunday

Today I'm thankful for:

Saturday

Small Acts of Kindness I can do this week:

Weekly Assignment:

Is there anyone I need to forgive so that I can have more freedom in my heart and move on?

Week

Weekly Inspiration:

"Gratitude is the sign of noble souls."

-Aesop

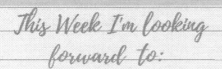

This Week I'm looking forward to:

Monday
Today I'm thankful for:

Tuesday
Today I'm thankful for:

Wednesday
Today I'm thankful for:

30

Today I'm thankful for:

Thursday

Today I'm thankful for:

Friday

Today I'm thankful for:

Sunday

Today I'm thankful for:

Saturday

Small Acts of Kindness I can do this week:

Weekly Assignment:

What is the best compliment I've ever received and why was it so significant?

Week

This Week I'm looking forward to:

Monday

Today I'm thankful for:

Tuesday

Today I'm thankful for:

Wednesday

Today I'm thankful for:

31

Today I'm thankful for:

Thursday

Today I'm thankful for:

Friday

Today I'm thankful for:

Sunday

Today I'm thankful for:

Saturday

Small Acts of Kindness I
can do this week:

Weekly Assignment:

Who is the person I most admire and
why:

Week

Weekly Inspiration:

"Joy is the simplest form of gratitude."

-Karl Barth

This Week I'm looking forward to:

Monday

Today I'm thankful for:

Tuesday

Today I'm thankful for:

Wednesday

Today I'm thankful for:

32

Today I'm thankful for:

Thursday

Today I'm thankful for:

Friday

Today I'm thankful for:

Sunday

Today I'm thankful for:

Saturday

Small Acts of Kindness I can do this week:

Weekly Assignment:

What's my favorite place in the world and why?

Week

"I know that when I pray, something wonderful happens. Not just to the person or persons for whom I'm praying, but also something wonderful happens to me. I'm grateful that I'm heard."

-Maya Angelou

This Week I'm looking forward to:

Monday

Today I'm thankful for:

Tuesday

Today I'm thankful for:

Wednesday

Today I'm thankful for:

33

Today I'm thankful for:

Thursday

Today I'm thankful for:

Friday

Today I'm thankful for:

Sunday

Today I'm thankful for:

Saturday

Small Acts of Kindness I
can do this week:

Weekly Assignment:

What's the best thing that happened

this week?

Week

Weekly Inspiration:

"The brave who focus on all things good and all things beautiful and all things true, even in the small, who give thanks for it and discover joy even in the here and now, they are the change agents who bring fullest Light to all the world."

-Ann Voskamp

This Week I'm looking forward to:

Monday
Today I'm thankful for:

Tuesday
Today I'm thankful for:

Wednesday
Today I'm thankful for:

34

Small Acts of Kindness I can do this week:

Today I'm thankful for:

Thursday

Today I'm thankful for:

Friday

Today I'm thankful for:

Sunday

Today I'm thankful for:

Saturday

Weekly Assignment:

What's my happiest childhood memory?

Week

Weekly Inspiration:

"Don't worry about anything; instead, pray about everything. Tell God what you need, and thank Him for all He has done. Then you will experience God's peace, which exceeds anything we can understand. His peace will guard your hearts and minds as you live in Christ Jesus."

-Philippians 4:6-7 (NLT)

This Week I'm looking forward to:

Monday
Today I'm thankful for:

Tuesday
Today I'm thankful for:

Wednesday
Today I'm thankful for:

35

Today I'm thankful for:

Thursday

Today I'm thankful for:

Friday

Today I'm thankful for:

Sunday

Today I'm thankful for:

Saturday

Small Acts of Kindness I can do this week:

Weekly Assignment:

Write about something good that happened today (or yesterday if it's morning):

Week

Weekly Inspiration:

"There's no happier person than a truly thankful, content person."

-Joyce Meyer

This Week I'm looking forward to:

Monday

Today I'm thankful for:

Tuesday

Today I'm thankful for:

Wednesday

Today I'm thankful for:

36

Today I'm thankful for:

Thursday

Today I'm thankful for:

Friday

Today I'm thankful for:

Sunday

Today I'm thankful for:

Saturday

Small Acts of Kindness I can do this week:

Weekly Assignment:
What's going on in my life right now, that I'm very grateful for?

Week

"Give thanks to the LORD, for He is good; His loving devotion endures forever."

- 1 Chronicles 16:34 (BSB)

This Week I'm looking forward to:

Monday
Today I'm thankful for:

Tuesday
Today I'm thankful for:

Wednesday
Today I'm thankful for:

37

Thursday

Today I'm thankful for:

Friday

Today I'm thankful for:

Sunday

Today I'm thankful for:

Saturday

Today I'm thankful for:

Small Acts of Kindness I can do this week:

Weekly Assignment:

Who is someone that inspires me and why?

Weekly Inspiration:

"He enjoys much who is thankful for little."

-Thomas Secker

This Week I'm looking forward to:

Monday

Today I'm thankful for:

Tuesday

Today I'm thankful for:

Wednesday

Today I'm thankful for:

38

Today I'm thankful for:

Thursday

Today I'm thankful for:

Friday

Today I'm thankful for:

Sunday

Today I'm thankful for:

Saturday

Small Acts of Kindness I can do this week:

Weekly Assignment:

What are 3 things that I appreciate

about where I live?

Week

"We are in a wrong state of mind if we are not in a thankful state of mind."

-Charles Spurgeon

This Week I'm looking forward to:

Monday

Today I'm thankful for:

Tuesday

Today I'm thankful for:

Wednesday

Today I'm thankful for:

39

Today I'm thankful for:

Thursday

Today I'm thankful for:

Friday

Today I'm thankful for:

Sunday

Today I'm thankful for:

Saturday

Small Acts of Kindness I can do this week:

Weekly Assignment:

What opportunities have I had in my life that I'm thankful for?

Week

"Enter His gates with thanksgiving and His Courts with praise! Give thanks to Him; bless His name!
For the Lord is good; His steadfast love endures forever, And His faithfulness to all generations."

-Psalm 100:4-5 (ESV)

This Week I'm looking forward to:

Monday
Today I'm thankful for:

Tuesday
Today I'm thankful for:

Wednesday
Today I'm thankful for:

40

Today I'm thankful for:

Thursday

Today I'm thankful for:

Friday

Today I'm thankful for:

Sunday

Today I'm thankful for:

Saturday

Small Acts of Kindness I can do this week:

Weekly Assignment:

If I could relive any moment, what would it be and why?

Week

Weekly Inspiration:

"I am beginning to learn that it is the sweet, simple things of life which are the real ones after all."

-Laura Ingalls Wilder

This Week I'm looking forward to:

Monday

Today I'm thankful for:

Tuesday

Today I'm thankful for:

Wednesday

Today I'm thankful for:

41

Today I'm thankful for:

Thursday

Today I'm thankful for:

Friday

Today I'm thankful for:

Sunday

Today I'm thankful for:

Saturday

Small Acts of Kindness I can do this week:

Weekly Assignment:

Write about a time I was blessed by kindness of another person:

Week

"The Lord is close to all who call on Him, yes, to all who call on Him in truth."

-Psalm 145:18 (NLT)

This Week I'm looking forward to:

Monday

Today I'm thankful for:

Tuesday

Today I'm thankful for:

Wednesday

Today I'm thankful for:

42

Today I'm thankful for:

Thursday

Today I'm thankful for:

Friday

Today I'm thankful for:

Sunday

Today I'm thankful for:

Saturday

Small Acts of Kindness I can do this week:

Weekly Assignment:

Reflect on a situation that changed my life for better.

Week

This Week I'm looking forward to:

Monday

Today I'm thankful for:

Tuesday

Today I'm thankful for:

Wednesday

Today I'm thankful for:

43

Today I'm thankful for:

Thursday

Today I'm thankful for:

Friday

Today I'm thankful for:

Sunday

Today I'm thankful for:

Saturday

Small Acts of Kindness I can do this week:

Weekly Assignment:

Something different today than it was from a year ago, that I'm very grateful for:

Week

"Most important of all, continue to show deep love for each other, for love covers a multitude of sins."

-1 Peter 4:8 (NLT)

This Week I'm looking forward to:

Monday
Today I'm thankful for:

Tuesday
Today I'm thankful for:

Wednesday
Today I'm thankful for:

44

Today I'm thankful for:

Thursday

Today I'm thankful for:

Friday

Today I'm thankful for:

Sunday

Today I'm thankful for:

Saturday

Small Acts of Kindness I can do this week:

Weekly Assignment:

Something that was once a struggle for me, but no longer is:

Week

Weekly Inspiration:

"We must accept finite disappointment, but never lose infinite hope."

- Martin Luther King Jr.

This Week I'm looking forward to:

Monday

Today I'm thankful for:

Tuesday

Today I'm thankful for:

Wednesday

Today I'm thankful for:

45

Today I'm thankful for:

Thursday

Today I'm thankful for:

Friday

Today I'm thankful for:

Sunday

Today I'm thankful for:

Saturday

Small Acts of Kindness I can do this week:

Weekly Assignment:

Reflection time: Is there anyone I need to forgive and let go so I can walk in more freedom?

Weekly Inspiration:

"But those who trust in the Lord for help will find their strength renewed. They will rise on wings like eagles, they will run and not get weary; they will walk and not grow weak."

-Isaiah 40:31 (GNT)

Week

This Week I'm looking forward to:

Monday

Today I'm thankful for:

Tuesday

Today I'm thankful for:

Wednesday

Today I'm thankful for:

46

Today I'm thankful for:

Thursday

Today I'm thankful for:

Friday

Today I'm thankful for:

Sunday

Today I'm thankful for:

Saturday

Small Acts of Kindness I can do this week:

Weekly Assignment:

Something I've done that's blessed another person:

Week

"Love begins at home, and it is not how much we do... but how much love we put in that action."

- Mother Teresa

This Week I'm looking forward to:

Monday

Today I'm thankful for:

Tuesday

Today I'm thankful for:

Wednesday

Today I'm thankful for:

47

Today I'm thankful for:

Thursday

Today I'm thankful for:

Friday

Today I'm thankful for:

Sunday

Today I'm thankful for:

Saturday

Small Acts of Kindness I can do this week:

Weekly Assignment:

What lessons have I learned that I'm thankful for?

Weekly Inspiration:

"Come to Me, all you who are weary and burdened, and I will give you rest. Take My yoke upon you and learn from Me, for I am gentle and humble in heart, and you will find rest for your souls. For my yoke is easy and my burden is light." - Jesus

Matthew 11:28-30 (NIV)

This Week I'm looking forward to:

Monday

Today I'm thankful for:

Tuesday

Today I'm thankful for:

Wednesday

Today I'm thankful for:

48

Today I'm thankful for:

Thursday

Today I'm thankful for:

Friday

Today I'm thankful for:

Sunday

Today I'm thankful for:

Saturday

Small Acts of Kindness I can do this week:

Weekly Assignment:

What 5 things do I love most about my family?

Weekly Inspiration:

"When trouble comes, focus on God's ability to care for you."

-Charles Stanley

This Week I'm looking forward to:

Monday

Today I'm thankful for:

Tuesday

Today I'm thankful for:

Wednesday

Today I'm thankful for:

49

Today I'm thankful for:

Thursday

Today I'm thankful for:

Friday

Today I'm thankful for:

Sunday

Today I'm thankful for:

Saturday

Small Acts of Kindness I can do this week:

Weekly Assignment:

what's my favorite memory and why?

Week

Weekly Inspiration:

"Start by doing what's necessary; then do what's possible; and suddenly you are doing the impossible."

- Francis of Assisi

This Week I'm looking forward to:

Monday
Today I'm thankful for:

Tuesday
Today I'm thankful for:

Wednesday
Today I'm thankful for:

50

Today I'm thankful for:

Thursday

Today I'm thankful for:

Friday

Today I'm thankful for:

Sunday

Today I'm thankful for:

Saturday

Small Acts of Kindness I can do this week:

Weekly Assignment:

Look around the room/ home and list

5 things I'm thankful for:

Week

Weekly Inspiration:

Faith makes all things possible... love makes all things easy".

- Dwight L. Moody

This Week I'm looking forward to:

Monday
Today I'm thankful for:

Tuesday
Today I'm thankful for:

Wednesday
Today I'm thankful for:

51

Today I'm thankful for:

Thursday

Today I'm thankful for:

Friday

Today I'm thankful for:

Sunday

Today I'm thankful for:

Saturday

Small Acts of Kindness I can do this week:

Weekly Assignment:

Write a list of dreams and goals I have for this next year of my life:

Week

This Week I'm looking forward to:

Monday

Today I'm thankful for:

Tuesday

Today I'm thankful for:

Wednesday

Today I'm thankful for:

52

Today I'm thankful for:

Thursday

Today I'm thankful for:

Friday

Today I'm thankful for:

Sunday

Today I'm thankful for:

Saturday

Small Acts of Kindness I can do this week:

Weekly Assignment:

Reflect on what I've learned on this journey of growing in gratitude. How am I different than I was a year ago?

Made in the USA
Columbia, SC
13 November 2020